Patricia Marne is a gra
and Chairwoman of
leading expert in the
recruitment and perso
gation and other lega
published many artic
books, most recently
writing (Macdonald Optima, 1991).

0689- 33581

H S mith

Demo I. C. D.
0932 254654

THE
CRIMINAL
HAND

AN ANALYSIS OF
CRIMINAL HANDWRITING

Patricia Marne

SPHERE BOOKS LIMITED

A Sphere Book

First published in Great Britain in 1991 by Sphere Books,
a Division of Macdonald & Co (Publishers),
London & Sydney

ISBN 0 7474 0953 6

Typeset in ITC Cheltenham by Leaper & Gard Ltd, Bristol.
Printed in Great Britain by Cox & Wyman Ltd, Reading.

Sphere Books Ltd
A Division of
Macdonald & Co (Publishers) Ltd
Orbit House
1 New Fetter Lane
London EC4A 1AR
A member of Maxwell Macmillan Pergamon Publishing Corporation

Contents

'Give me two lines of a man's handwriting
and I will hang him.'

Cardinal Richelieu

Author's note

Although the ancient Chinese and Romans accepted that there was a relationship between handwriting and personality, it was not until comparatively recently that graphology could lay claim to being a science with clearly defined rules and findings accurate enough to be used in commerce and industry, criminal detection and personality assessment. Furthermore, serious practitioners have had to fight against popular misconceptions that associate graphology with the occult.

Until the late middle ages, learning to write was the prerogative of monks and the aristocracy, and it was not until the practice of writing became part of everyday life that graphology started to come into its own. Some two hundred years ago graphologists were of two schools, one intuitive, the other analytical. The intuitive school would assess handwriting from the general impression it gave (its form level) while the analytical school studied what they termed 'isolated signs' and individual idiosyncracies of letter formation.

Gradually there were those who integrated these two, and in the nineteenth and twentieth centuries psychologists such as Max Pulver and Carl Jung added a new dimension to graphology by seeing symbols in handwriting that could reveal the subconscious drives of the writer. Today as a result of this and other research it is accepted that handwriting can get nearer the truth about an individual than shrewd, prolonged questioning.

Because graphology reveals the submerged personality and the hidden weaknesses and strengths of the writer, it enables the graphologist to determine with authority, the character of the writer, his disposition, educational development, emotional and mental faculties, and the influences that may affect him from both emotional and environmental experiences. The graphologist is able to interpret quickly and objectively, often confirming the opinion of psychologists and criminologists.

Introduction

This book is concerned with one specialised area: criminal tendencies and inclinations as revealed in handwriting. These are shown by a wide variety of tell-tale signs, but no graphologist would describe a person dishonest or criminal just on the strength of one or two of these give-away clues, any more than a physician would diagnose a particular illness without taking more than one symptom into account.

Even when the presence of a particular characteristic has been confirmed, the graphologist will balance it against other characteristics. A particular handwriting may show clear signs that two individuals are thieves, but further study will show that one is aggressive and the other is not. One, if caught, will attack and seriously injure his detector; the other will concede 'It's a fair cop' and go quietly. Before venturing into this specialised field it will be helpful first to define very briefly the technical knowledge which graphologists apply when studying any script.

All handwriting analysis is based on three zones: the upper zone shows the spiritual and intellectual state, the middle zone the social and day-to-day attitude, and the lower zone the materialistic and subconscious instincts, emotional and sex drives.

Ideally each zone should be the same size but this rarely happens. Where it does, the writing may seem dull and stereotyped.

If there is neglect of one zone or an exaggeration at the cost of others, this has a special significance and has to be taken into account.

Two factors which handwriting does not reveal with absolute certainty are age and gender. Before attempting an analysis, it is important to know these because some people at twenty are more mature than others at fifty. Everyone, too, has male and female characteristics in different proportions, both physically and psychologically.

Having noted the three zones, the graphologist then looks for further clues in:

- The slant
- Pressure and speed
- Script size and formation
- Base line (whether straight or wavering)
- Form level (whether high, medium, or low) – this is important for revealing intelligence
- Margins
- Spacing between letters, words and lines
- Capital letters
- Small letters
- The capital *I* and letter *t* bar crossing
- Loops, or lack of them
- Punctuation marks
- Signature
- Numerals

There are, of course, numerous finer points but where relevant they are mentioned later in following chapters.

GRAPHOLOGY AND THE LAW

Just as fingerprints studied by an expert can reveal the identity of a suspect, handwriting when analysed by an experienced graphologist can provide unmistakable clues in detecting criminal tendencies. Handwriting and fingerprints are both unique to their owner, but it has taken the judiciary in Britain longer to accept the value of graphology as evidence than it has in Europe. Scotland Yard and the CID of many other police forces will consider any leads when painstakingly sifting clues in tracking down wrong-doers, but rarely do they acknowledge publicly that they employ graphologists, prefering to call them handwriting experts.

The use of graphology by criminologists is by no means new, and as this book will show, there are many instances over the years where the study of handwriting has been used to reveal criminal or anti-social tendencies of men and women in notorious cases. A recent example is the analysis of the script of writers, usually anonymous, and sometimes hoaxers, in the 'Yorkshire Ripper' investigation.

1

Clues to criminal types

OPEN BASELINE TO SMALL a'S AND o'S

we cant find a way
=
getting any money
we can get it togetr

A cardinal sign of deceit is the open baseline to the small *a*'s and *o*'s. This is not only a sign of dishonesty but of hypocrisy, and shows the writer is not to be trusted. In this illustration the left slant and the thick pasty writing also point to dishonesty. The short heavy *t* bar crossing indicates a bad temper and the arcade writing of the small *m*'s and *n*'s (see page 13) are an added sign of a person who is deceitful.

WAVERING BASELINE

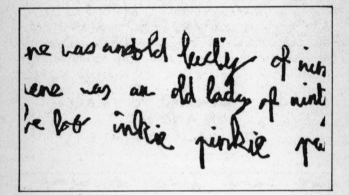

The wavering baseline, with its ups and downs and words running into each other, shows an erratic and disorderly mind, with inner conflict, and an individual who is anything but calm and composed. The writer is disturbed emotionally and the downward slope towards the end of the lines shows depression and pessimism.

VARIABLE SLANT

A varying slant means that the writer, although versatile, quickly loses interest and is erratic and mercurial. The *a*'s and *o*'s open at the top show that he is likely to be over-active and over-talkative and over-react in situations that call for self-control.

INFLATED CAPITALS

Inflated or exaggerated capitals are seen in the handwriting of people who love to be admired and who enjoy being the centre of attention. The egoist who seeks the limelight, the weak-willed and the inferiority complex are often hidden behind huge embellished capitals; they indicate the writer is far more interested in giving an impression, in showing off at all costs, even employing deceit at times, rather than being himself. They also have neurotic tendencies, as these capitals frequently show a narcissistic desire for grandeur, a weakness in many criminals.

LEFT TENDING STROKES TO CAPITALS

Left-tending strokes to capitals again indicate deceitfulness. When seen frequently, with long loops and reaching far to the left, it is an unmistakable sign of dishonesty.

This deceit may not always be criminal deceit but emotional, and it indicates a fair amount of vanity on the part of the writer.

ENROLLED CAPITALS

These are a cardinal sign of deceit.

SIGNATURES

If the signature is the same size as the rest of the script, this is usually a sign of reliability and honesty, and a desire to communicate clearly and distinctly. The writer does not put up any façade but is the same in private as in public.

When there is a discrepancy between signature and script and the signature is entirely different from the body of the writing, this can denote a dual nature and shows that the writer hides behind a mask and conceals his inner nature. See the signatures of Emil Savundra (p. 18) and Charles Manson (p. 55).

THREAD SCRIPT

This threadlike writing shows the opportunist, someone who knows how to manipulate and persuade, and also someone who is difficult, if not impossible, to pin down. Such writers are versatile and changeable, possess considerable talent in getting on with people, and have the ability to get their own way. They are quick thinking and able to make decisions.

They are all things to all people, and among these scripts we have the man who can adapt to any situation and turn it to his advantage.

This script is found among shrewd opportunists who are also clever and creative. But it may also be that of the dishonest salesman, the con man or the quick-witted, get-rich-quick businessman who preys on the gullible.

ARCADE WRITING

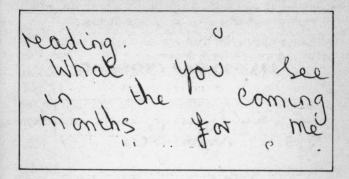

When letters are arched at the top in arcade fashion (note the small *m*'s and *n*'s) they reveal a personality who prefers to keep his thoughts to himself and is secretive, not necessarily to deceive, but through habit. The higher the arcade the more artistic the writer, the flatter the arcade the more of an intriguer. Arcade script which slants to the left reveals deceit, and this example also has a symbol of the pound sign, showing more than a passing interest in money.

FLAT SMALL m'S

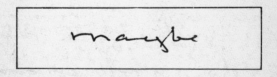

Small flat-topped m's and n's reveal the bluffer, the person who can usually talk or act his way out of difficult situations and who is lacking in normal moral standards.

This wide script shows extravagance and a lack of appreciation of the value of time or effort in everyday affairs. This and the light pressure shows the writer to be hyper-sensitive and critical of others.

LIAR'S † BAR CROSSING

This *t* bar coming down the stem and going over to the right shows the writer who will not hesitate to lie or use deceit to extricate himself from awkward situations in which he is at fault. The habitual liar often repeats this *t* bar throughout his script. In graphology this is regarded as one of the most revealing signs.

TOUCHING UP STROKES

Touching up and going over the strokes shows a neurotic personality, full of uncertainty, lacking in decisiveness and unreliable. These are not necessarily criminal traits but the obsessive necessity to add, strengthen or make legible his writing is a sign of neurosis caused by inner conflicts and anxiety.

LETTERS OMITTED

Letters that are omitted in handwriting reveal a poor memory and sometimes nervousness or anxiety. They are also seen in handwriting of dishonest people, and these slips of the pen may stem from inner conflicts – usually of guilt, as the writers are constantly on the lookout for detection.

PASTY WRITING

Pasty writing shows sensuality and is found in the handwriting of those who allow their appetites to rule and indulge in excessive eating, drinking and sex. It shows a preoccupation with the physical and reveals the force of energy the writer uses. When the writing is light and pasty the vitality is less than when it is heavy and muddy in appearance.

UNEVEN (PERIODIC) PRESSURE

Uneven or periodic pressure reveals irritability and a very uncertain temper under tension. The writer is easily excited and stimulated, and can be demanding in the sexual erotic area. Lack of emotional balance is also indicated, resulting sometimes in violent behaviour according to the heaviness of the pressure.

SPLIT LETTERS

> dont ever seem to
> get things clone

Letters that are split apart show dishonesty in money affairs. When accompanied by a left slant and arcade script, they are signs to be watched as the writer will also distort the truth. This sign shows weakness of will due to nervous anxiety and feelings of guilt.

Example 1:
THE CRIMINALLY DISHONEST

> about the job, I cant see how
> to make much of a success of

This writer's script shows four cardinal signs of dishonesty. Left slant, arcadé *m*'s and *n*s, an open base for the small *a*'s and *o*'s and enrolled capitals.

The large loop to the small *h* reveals a slightly muddle-headed personality, and the slow ponderous writing a lack of mental agility.

Emil Savundra was a financier who spent several years in prison in connection with insurance frauds. An outstanding characteristic of his writing, shown here, is the discrepancy between the signature and the text. The small writing shows mental agility, the exaggerated capital *I* his ego, and the large upward-rising underlined signature shows his self-love, ambition and desire for greatness, prestige and position.

Example 2:
THE PSYCHOPATHIC CRIMINAL

I'm sat on my bunk. Everything in my cell is very still. I like it in here. Without anyone ragging me and probbing my mind. I just sit here in my fantasy **HIDE** looking at these bars keeping me in. I don't suppose if they weren't on I'd run.

IN MY SHELL

I MAGINE

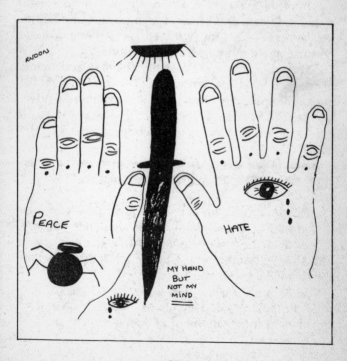

This woman aged 23 has a history of violence, including grievous bodily harm, breaking and entering, assault and carrying a deadly weapon. Her handwriting and drawings are fascinating graphic symbols of her immaturity and psychopathic personality.

She killed an eleven-year-old child when she herself was just eleven years old, stabbing the other girl with a knife, but ran away and was not suspected of the crime. Her emotional and environmental background was one of domestic upsets, rows, arguments, a drunken father and a weak mother, neglected children, two brothers in trouble with the police before they were nine, and aggression.

After the killing, she left home and lived rough, sleeping in cars and breaking into houses and factories, always — as she stressed — carrying a knife because she did not feel dressed without it.

She had nightmares about the killing, black moods of despair and depression and even thought of ending her own life. She was eventually apprehended, and sent to borstal. At the age of 21 she was a hardened criminal and still very much hung up about the murder.

Some of her drawings illustrate her terror, depression and guilt, her persecution complex and her schizoid nature.

Her writing with its copybook form level and lack of originality shows immaturity and this is also revealed in the underlengths to her small g and y with their leftward swing. This shows her impressionability and lack of maturity.

The flat wide small m's and n's are a sign that she is not forthcoming and is able to bluff her way out of uncomfortable situations. The loops to the small k

indicate rebelliousness. The fullness of a few upper loops shows that she is capable of emotion, but the slanting to the left prevents her from expressing this easily.

There is a lack of consistency in the periodic pressure which indicates sudden and unexpected outbursts of temper due to frustration. The fluctuating base line and slant reveal her emotional and mental instability.

However, the capital *I*, straight down and without any embellishment or ornamentation, shows that she can get down quickly to essentials and sum up a situation. The elongated dashes above the *i* stem show a quick and sensitive temper which flares up hastily.

Her preoccupation with knives is symbolic of her disturbed mind. This symbol is repeated over and over again, sometimes heavily dripping with blood, nearly always filled in and with heavy pressure.

The anger, frustration and feelings of unworthiness are seen in the beetles, and despair and depression are shown in the watching eyes which are an indication of suspicion. These frequently appear in the doodles of paranoid personalities.

This woman is preoccupied with death, destruction, suicide, anger and hate.

Example 3:
THE CRIMINALLY INSANE

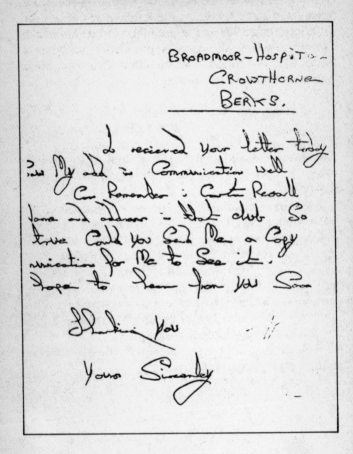

This writer was judged criminally insane. The curious unusual upper loops, nicked and slanting to the left show he is unrealistic and does not come down to earth.

Such a person lives in his own private world of fantasy, often in a state of exaltation for which there is lack of reason or logic. The large and frequent use of capitals is often seen in the handwriting of writers suffering from delusions of grandeur or megalomania. The writers lack all sense of proportion and rarely leave the institutions where they live out their fantasies.

2

A gallery of murderers

Murder is the ultimate crime that one person can commit against another, and it arouses deep interest and curiosity — not always morbid — because people are intrigued about the personality of the killer. Although graphology can reveal the character and motivation of a killer, there is no such thing as 'a murderer's handwriting'.

Every person who kills for whatever purpose has an entirely different script — there are no two handwritings the same — but there are certain specific signs that point to possible future violence. For instance, ungovernable rage, hot temper and sadistic tendencies are all characteristics that can be seen in the script as warning signs.

The rape murderer will reveal strong sexual desires (see Cambridge Rapist) which cannot be controlled, but each murderer is an individual whose handwriting must be examined to determine just what inner compulsion resulted in the taking of a life.

Most murders are domestic murders committed within the family in a moment of anger or passion, and by ordinary people. Until recently there were few murders in this country committed during robbery, but now this crime is on the increase, and a new ruthless kind of killer for gain is emerging. Whether murderers belong to the first category or the second does not mean that they have the same or similar handwriting.

The psychopath is perhaps the most cold-blooded of all murderers because he may have little motive for killing and will exhibit no sense of guilt. His handwriting often shows extreme tension, anger and pent-up emotional rage that can smoulder quietly for years without erupting. His external attitude may be pleasant and normal on the surface, hiding his inner aggression so well that he is rarely suspected of being the anti-social person that he is. His handwriting will have positive traits as well as negative, and he is, of all criminals, the hardest to detect even from his handwriting.

He is mentally ill but not insane, and this definition is by itself confusing. His handwriting will reveal characteristics that taken together point to immaturity, emotional isolation and preoccupation with self, a low tolerance level, strong feelings of rejection, an abnormal interest in sex, and a lack of identity, all characteristic traits of the psychopathic killer.

Very often there are other clues in the form of strong emotional and environmental hang-ups from past experiences, usually of rejection by one or both parents in the formative years.

You will doubtless have
told you that I have
arranged for patent
renewal fees and
all matters thereto to
be cared for for so
long as I am unable
to do so personally.

Also the Walpole
Investment Trust.

It is with joy that I
remember those
heavens that I have
known in the many
happy days that I
have spent with you:
the most wonderful

family that any man
could be privileged
to know.

My love to you all
John.

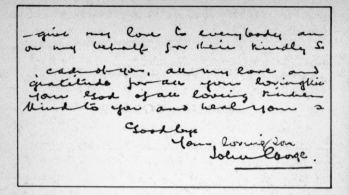

Haigh was known as the Acid Bath Murderer because of his method of disposing of his victims' bodies in a bath of acid. He was hanged in Brixton prison in 1946 and was believed to have killed at least five people for their money and property.

At first sight his handwriting is attractive, being well spaced, smooth and flowing, but closer examination gives a different picture. The thread formations show his talent for manipulating people for his own ends, and his capacity for being all things to all men.

He was not highly sexed, as demonstrated by the straight downstrokes of his *g*'s and *y*'s while the upright script indicates that his head ruled his heart and that he had plenty of self-control. The open small *a*'s and *o*'s are a sign of eloquence. The fluctuating pressure nevertheless, shows instability and that the writer was living under considerable tension.

The 'garland' script (as the *m* in 'family') shows his almost feminine personality and indicates that he could get along well with elderly women.

His signature shows that he was subject to strong environmental and emotional influences from the past, and that he was still affected by these links and ties. His enrolled small *s*'s show shrewdness and a calculating mind.

Haigh was a clever and shrewd opportunist who was also a strategist … in murder.

WILLIAM CORDER

William was the perpetrator of the infamous Red Barn murder; named thus because the victim, Maria Martin, was found buried in a barn in Polstead, Suffolk. Corder made a written confession before he was hanged on 11 August 1828 in front of the gaol at Bury St Edmunds, before a huge crowd.

The blotchy script shows sensuality and the varying pressure indicates unpredictable moods. The long *t* bars that cover the entire words, show a domineering and forceful nature, and the angular formations of many small letters, particularly the *n* and *m*, indicate aggression and energy. The spacing is small and rushes towards the right margin, indicating that he had an almost pathological need to be with people. The high aggressive stroke to his capital *M* in Mother, confirms his aggressiveness.

WILLIAM GARDINER

D R

I will try to see you tonight at 12 o'clock at your Place if you Put a light in your window at 10 oclock for about 10 minutes then you can take it out again. dont have a light in your Room at 12 as I will come round to the back

William Gardiner was a Suffolk carpenter, a rather pious Elder of the Methodist church, nicknamed Holy Willie. Gossip linked him with Rose Harsent, a 23-year-old maid in the household of a Baptist deacon. As a result he was summoned to appear before the church elders.

Rose was subsequently found dead, her throat cut and her body partly burned. A medicine bottle with traces of paraffin and bearing the names of two of Gardiner's children was found, and in Rose's bedroom an unsigned note of assignation. She was six months pregnant.

Gardiner was tried in Ipswich in 1902. His wife swore he was with her all through the night of the murder, save for half an hour, at about 11.30 p.m. She said she had given the medicine bottle containing camphorated oil to Rose, who had a cold. The jury failed to agree and a new trial was ordered. Again the jury could not agree and Gardiner was released.

The most important aspects of Gardiner's handwriting are its neatness, the small script and the regular spacing, all of which are evidence of a conventional normal person. But the threadlike strokes which almost dissolve are a cardinal sign of the opportunist and the personality who knows how to manipulate and get his own way. He was able to use his considerable elusiveness to gain his own ends and wriggle out of responsibility.

DR WILLIAM PALMER

I last saw you I have
not had two hours
sleep I do assure you I
never felt so tired in my
life. I am almost sick
of my Profession — Sorry
I am to say my Mother
has had another attack
& one of my Sisters
children I think will
be dead before morning
it is now 1/2 p 10 I have just
came home from Hay to
write you for I do assure you
my dearest I should have
been very unhappy had I
not have done so.
My dearest Annie I
purpose all being well

being with you tomorrow
about three & depend
upon it nothing but
ill health will ever
keep me away from
you — forgive me my
duck for not sending
you the paper last
night I really could
not help it — I will
explain fully tomorrow
my dear remember I say
something about needle
work — you will be amused
My sweetest & loveliest
Annie I never was more
pleased with you in my
life than I was on Friday

Dr Palmer was the notorious English poisoner of possibly fourteen people. His trial in 1856 made legal history because the inquest into the death of his last victim returned a verdict of wilful murder against him even before he was arrested. This led to the Palmer Act making it possible for an accused person to be tried in London if he was unlikely to get a fair trial in his own county. Palmer was subsequently hanged.

Palmer's middle zone handwriting shows his intellectual capacity for assessing facts. The thread script also reveals his talent for manipulating them. The lack of clear spacing between words is a sign of gregariousness. Unlike many murderers, he preferred to have people around him and was not a loner, but the long *t* bar roofing his words here and there is an indication of his patronising attitude to others. His wide right margin reveals apprehension about the future.

HAWLEY HARVEY CRIPPEN

I cannot stand the horrors I go
every night any longer and as I
nothing bright ahead and money
come to an end I have made
my mind to jump overboard to
I know I have spoil your life
I hope someday you can learn t
nie with last words of love you

Crippen was an American, born in Michigan in 1852, who qualified as a doctor, and came to England in 1900, but his qualifications did not allow him to practise.

He and his mistress Ethel le Neve, who was disguised as a boy, had fled the country after Crippen was suspected of murdering his wife. They were detained on board ship following radio messages from London, the first time radio had ever been used in crime detection. Crippen was subsequently convicted and hanged. Ethel le Neve was acquitted.

The threadlike strokes in Crippen's writing show his talent for using people to his own advantage, and the very large capitals reveal an inferiority complex. But the right slant shows him to be sociable and able to communicate and mix with people. The formation of his small *p*'s with their pointed downstrokes, indicate his lack of domestic harmony.

His signature with its right slant shows his passionate and ardent nature, and the heavier pressure used in this signature shows his desire for prestige and for people to think well of him.

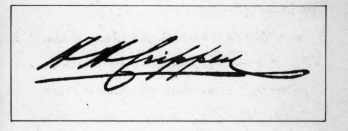

HERBERT ROWSE ARMSTRONG

Herbert Armstrong was a small town solicitor and retired British Army major who was hanged in 1922 for the murder of his wife by poisoning. His wife's death did not at first attract attention but later, when he attempted to poison a rival solicitor, his wife's body was exhumed and a post mortem conducted by Bernard Spilsbury. The case aroused considerable public interest at the time.

His writing shows a very strong ego as evidenced in the larger-than-normal script signature, heavy underlining and heavy pressure. This pressure shows his energy, while the thick *t* bar crossing indicates obstinacy and persistence which could find expression in an explosion of pent-up anger. He had a sadistic streak of refined brutality, as shown by the elongated *i* dots. The spacing shows the writer thinks first before acting and is capable of carefully and meticulously calculating his moves.

Number	Name		
		Gloucester	Prison
		30 May	1922

My dear Matthews.

My heart was too full today to say all I wished. Thank you, my friend, for all you have done for me. No one could have done more. Please convey also to all your Staff my gratitude for the unnecessary work they put in. No team could have worked more loyally or with more devotion to duty

Ever yours faithful friend

H Rowse Armstrong

RONALD BENNELL

ANDY I want YOU TO tell TELL
THE FIRM TO SEND MY WAGES
HOME TO MY PARENTS, I THINK
I KILLED THAT GIRL BUT I AM
NOT SURE, BUT ITS MY RING
THEY FOUND, SO IT MUST BE ME,
TELL THE COPS NOT TO
LOOK FOR ME BECAUSE I WILL
KILL MYSELF

RON

Ronald Bennell, aged 18 years, was convicted in 1969 at Swanage, Dorset, for the rape and murder of 18-year-old Diana Stephanie Kemp.

This letter, written by Bennell, shows that he is semi-literate and extremely anxious. This is seen in the crossing out and over-stroking of letters. The varying slant and periodic pressure are indications of mental and emotional instability, and the large spacing between words shows that he is inclined to be a loner.

The writing also has a pastiness often seen in the script of the sexually excitable and sensual individual who has difficulty in keeping his instinctive urges under control.

Wallace was charged with the murder of his wife in 1930 in Liverpool. He was found guilty on circumstantial evidence, but on appeal he was cleared and left the court a free man. Wallace was 50, an insurance agent, quiet, inoffensive, intelligent and a member of the local chess club.

At first glance Wallace's handwriting is that of a well-balanced personality with mental alertness showing in the small script and tidy spacing. But there are four other traits shown which are conflicting. He was timid and introverted, as shown in insignificant *I* revealing an inferiority complex. But he had a certain amount of concealed ego: the capital letters are inflated compared with the rest of the script, and the capital *M* with its downstroke turning right shows his vanity and that he would resent any interference in his affairs. The heavy *t* bar crossings going downwards are a sign of an aggressive, domineering and argumentative personality with an awkward temper under stress. The capital *B* is a significant sexual symbol in his writing, as it goes down into the lower zone. This, combined with the narrow downstrokes of his *g*'s and *y*'s, shows that he was sexually frustrated, and his emotional needs had been neglected. His handwriting provides some interesting sidelights into the personality of a complex character.

Latham House
Grange-over-Sands
= Lancs.

Dear Mr Munro.
=   5/6/31.

Many thanks for your letter
and Bill of Costs to hand to-day.
=   It is a pretty formidable
document and as you say the total costs are
undoubtedly heavy. £1500 to establish an
innocent man's innocence does not seem
much like justice, but, there it is.
          I am completely satisfied that my
case could not have been in better hands, and
I know the amount of work put in by yourselves
has been really great. what I do object to is
that the damnable stupidity of the Lpool C.I.D.
should have made it necessary. Still, I'm free
again and that means everything.
          I will get into touch with our
Staff Federation and see what they have to
say. You will I am sure realise that
I am anxious to have a settlement
reached as early as possible and if there should
be some slight delay I will do what I can
to expedite matters.

          with kindest regards.
                    Very sincerely yours
                         WH Wallace

41

CHARLES FREDERICK PEACE

Sir. I am that most rected unhappy man John Ward. or Charles Peace but have Pity upon Me & let Me have a reply from you respacted Sir

Peace was one of the most notorious criminals and murderers of his age. He was born in 1832, was small and ugly but very agile and unusually strong. He became a master of disguise, and with theatrical flair he carried his housebreaking tools in a violin case. He shot a policeman and later the husband of a woman who had responded to his advances. He confessed to his crimes while awaiting execution, and was hanged in Leeds Prison in 1879. Many street ballads were written about him.

His script shows him to be almost illiterate, but the speed indicates a quick mind and ready wit. The high strokes to his small *p*'s show an enterprising nature and the long *t* bars reveal obstinacy and conceit. Some of the *t* bars have a symbolically shaped knife which reveal an unpredictable and unpleasant temper.

The uneven pressure is a sign of mood variation and instability. The *i* dot in 'sir', in the form of a small arc, demonstrates his quick and acute perception.

The left swing of his small *g*'s and *y*'s reveal that in his early life there was a strong, maybe dominant, mother influence.

LORD LUCAN

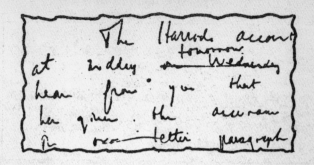

Lord Lucan is the peer the police want to interview following the murder of his children's nanny in 1974.

His small script reveals intelligence, and that he was under pressure at the time of writing. The over-strokes on some of his letters indicate neurotic tendencies, although the letters and their formation show self-control which may become weaker as feelings of persecution are magnified; this is seen in the widening left margin.

The threadlike script indicates his persuasive tongue and the knowledge of how to use it. The wavering pressure and ticklike stroke at the end of his downstrokes, show aggression and variation of his mood.

DR BUCK RUXTON

Dr Ruxton was a 37-year-old Parsee doctor who in 1928 set up house in Lancaster with Isabella van Ess, who called herself Mrs Ruxton.

In 1935 Mrs Ruxton and her maid disappeared. Ruxton reported that she had left him for another man. After the recovery of parts of their bodies, Ruxton was charged with their murder, found guilty and hanged at Strangeways Prison in 1936.

Ruxton's writing, with its heavy pressure and pasty script, reveals strong physical appetite. The thick *t* bars show brutal temper under tension and the formation of his capital *R*'s with their strokes going far down into the lower zone area indicates his unwillingness to compromise and an adamant attitude. The long stroke beginning the word 'Mary' shows inflated egoism and conceit.

> Lancaster.
> 14. 10. 35.
>
> I killed Mrs Ruxton in a fit of temper because I thought she had been with a man. I was Mad at the time. Mary Rogerson was present at the time. I had to Kill her.
>
> B Ruxton

DONALD NEILSON
(THE BLACK PANTHER)

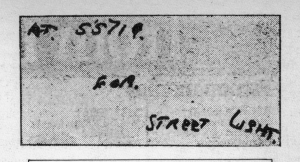

Donald Neilson, aged 38, was convicted of the murder of Leslie Whittle in 1975. Neilson, known as the Black Panther after shooting a security guard, left behind in an abandoned car several envelopes bearing his handwriting.

His writing is thick, with heavy pressure which shows aggression and brutality, and he has an eccentric habit of putting full stops between the letters when they are unnecessary. His writing — in capitals — reveals fluctuating pressure, which is a sign of emotional instability and often anger. The over-stroking of letters is a neurotic sign, which with a wavering baseline shows a personality lacking in balance to such an extent that the writer is danger-ously antisocial.

The large *C* shows that he has an exaggerated ego, while the pasty script reveals an earthy, materialistic nature. The sharpness of the capital *L*, at the end of Walsall, is a sign of aggression as are the hooks on his capital *W*.

From hell

Mr Lusk

Sor

I send you half the
Kidne I took from one women
prasarved it for you tother piece I
fried and ate it was very nise I
may send you the bloody knif that
took it out if you only wate a whil
longer

Signed   Catch me when
                you Can
             Mishter Lusk

Old boss you was — it was
he left Kidny i was goin to
hoperate agin clos to your
ospitle just as i was goin
to dror mi nife along of
er bloomin throte them
cusses of coppers spoilt
the game but i guess i will
be on the job soon and will
send you another bit of
innerds   jack the ripper

O have you seen the devle
with his mikerscope and scalpul
a lookin at a kidney
with a slide cocked up

This pasty, rather 'smudgy' or 'dirty' writing is from a letter believed to have been written by the original Whitechapel murderer known as 'Jack the Ripper'. It is completely chaotic in form and erratic in rhythm.

The long downstrokes to his small *g* and *y* are a sign of aggression, the periodic pressure reveals anger with emotional instability, leading to violent mood variation. The pointed *t* bars with their symbols of knives or daggers in the cross bar and their sharpening points indicate, and are symbolic of, the murder weapons used to mutilate victims.

The 'blobbing' of the ink is a sign of sensuality. The muddled and jumbled lines with the letters running into each other demonstrate inability to control intense emotion.

PETER KURTEN

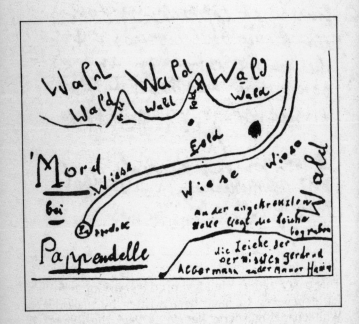

This 47-year-old German factory worker was a great admirer of Jack the Ripper. He was called the Monster of Dusseldorf after being caught by accident, and was charged with nine murders, sadistic killings of young children and girls committed between 1928–1930.

This map he drew shows the areas where he found his victims. The very heavy and pasty strokes reveal his intense sensuality and the filled-in writing shows a cruel sexual appetite. There is vanity in the over-large capitals and Kurten was, in fact, described by his wife as an exceedingly vain man. He was guillotined in Cologne in 1931.

PETER SUTCLIFFE

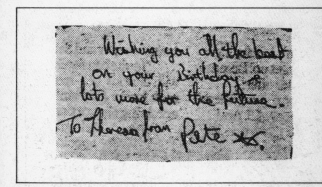

Peter William Sutcliffe the 34-year-old Bradford lorry driver known as the 'Yorkshire Ripper' was jailed for life in May 1981 after being found guilty of murdering 13 women and attempting to murder 7 more.

Sutcliffe was sentenced to serve at least 30 years

and to be released only on licence. Most of the women he killed were prostitutes, Sutcliffe claiming that he had a 'divine mission' to slaughter them after hearing voices in a Bingley cemetery while working as a grave-digger. His pleas of not guilty through diminished responsibility were rejected by a jury vote of 10 to 2.

The left slant to Sutcliffe's handwriting reveals his introverted nature and shows that he leads an active inner life. From the pressure it is obvious that he also suffers from depression. The rising lines of the writing signify undue optimism at times. The left slant also shows that he has strong emotional and environmental ties from his formative years which influence him and which he finds difficulty in breaking. He also has a strong attachment to his mother who had a lot of influence on him, leading to a curious love/hate relationship. The left strokes only half-looped reveal that he was dominated by his mother (it was established later that he was extremely fond of his mother).

Sutcliffe has a habit of adding little tiny drawings of of faces between his words, often a sign of mental abberation. The blotchy and fluctuating pressure of his writing shows his uncertain moods and sensuality. Yet the underlengths of his small *y*'s and *g*'s — sexual indications in handwriting analysis — reveal that he is weak in this area and afraid of women.

The capital *I* made in two strokes is an aggressive sign and the size demonstrates his feelings of inadequacy and inferiority, compensated for by acts of violence.

He writes the word GOD larger than the rest of the script. This is a 'motive' word, giving clues to his mental balance — in this instance he claimed to have heard voices from God when committing his

₄RK TRANSPORT

EVERANCE IRONWORKS

Nº 06660

'LEY

ıone 54031 day
    598427 night

Date MON 9TH NOV 79

~~COLLECT~~ / DELIVER
(delete when not applicable)

TINATION	DESCRIPTION
W/FRO BLENKINSOP LTD HALEBANK FACTORY LOWER RD WIDNESS CHESHIRE	140 DRUMS CHEMICALS 77,42 KGS.

	Tons	Cwts	Qtrs	lbs
No. FH0 21KS				
'ER'S NAME PN Sutcliffe				
‾ ARRIVAL 8-10 Am				
DEP. 10 45. Am				
. TIMES 12.30 - 10 PM				

51

Dear Tracy,

I thought about it
& I just had to drop you a line, I
was totally in sympathy with you
about what happened & you did the
right thing you know, I'm only sorry
that you had to endure the 3 or 4
days in that terrible place! I have to
admire the way you would go through
it again as a matter of principal" &
its chiefly why I've written, because
believe me, I mean, a have experienced
the kind of stitch up tactics &
pressure that you encountered. Simply
as one human being to another gal-
-justice is always clouded by bias &
innuendo!! Justice is Heaven sent &

numerous crimes. The spasmodic pressure signifies
his reactions are varying and inconsistent.

The lines going through his signature in a back-
ward formation are highly significant as they reveal

from nowhere else! I sincerely hope
that you are not required again in
such a capacity, & wish you all
the happiness & contentment life can
possibly offer you for the future!!

GOD Bless & take care!

My sincere regards

from Peter.

hostility to self — a cancelling out of the ego — and a
suicide sign in graphology. Self-destruction urges are
frequently found in handwriting either as a cry for
help by the writer or as a genuine bid for death.

PAUL JOHN KNOWLES

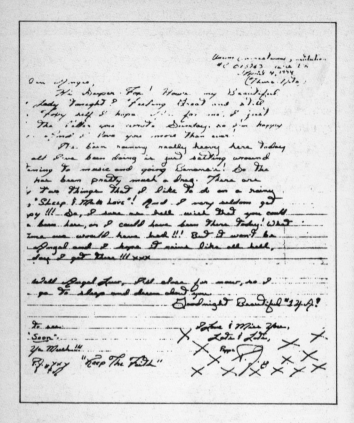

Knowles was an American escaped convict, who killed at least 15 people in a four-month period in 1975. All the victims were seemingly selected at random and most were killed brutally. After his arrest and whilst being transferred from one gaol to another, he managed to free one hand from his handcuffs and went for the driver's gun. Knowles was shot dead by one of the escorting police officers.

His writing shows a pronounced right slant showing his lack of emotional control and the strong leftward swing of his small *g*'s indicate a mother complex leading to suppressed homosexual tendencies.

The writing is pasty which is a sign of sensuality and strong physical urges, and the whiplike strokes going up and over to the left on the ending of many words is a sign of self-blame and guilt. They are also symbolic of his liking for ropes to tie up his victims.

CHARLES MANSON

Charles Manson was the leader of the so-called 'Family' whose brutal killings in California in August 1969 were followed by a sensational trial, in which

Manson and three girl followers were tried for seven murders. All four were found guilty and sentenced to death, which meant life imprisonment.

The pronounced left slant to Manson's writing reveals his basically introverted nature which is a barrier between himself and the real world.

The low *t* bars indicate a depressive personality and the discrepancy between his script and signature indicates his dual nature with an urge to be regarded as someone important. The small insignificant writing and the larger erratic and unstable signature without any rhythm show his personal imbalance. The angular strokes to his signature and narrow strokes are a sign of aggression and latent resentment.

MARK CHAPMAN

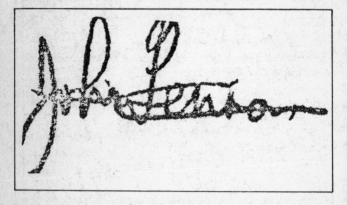

Mark Chapman killed Beatle John Lennon in New York on 1 December 1980. Chapman, 25 years old and a security guard, was a Beatle fan and believed that *he* was Lennon and that the real Beatle was an impostor, so shot him at point-blank range.

Chapman's 'Lennon' signature, with the lines scored through it, is a classic sign in graphology of the would-be suicide. Hostility to self is shown by his cancelling out of the ego, and this type of graphic symbol is often seen in the handwriting of disturbed individuals. When the line is weak and does not go all the way through the signature, it can be a cry for help; when the signature is circled all the way around, it indicates strong suicidal and/or homicidal tendencies.

The inhibited letters and heavy pressure indicate his tension and highly emotional state at the time of writing.

WILLIAM HEIRENS

For heavens
SAke catch me
Before I kill more
I cannot control
myself

Heirens, an American, brought up to believe that sexual relations were unclean, found sexual gratification in burglary and murder. By the age of 13 he had committed 11 burglaries and set fire to six houses. As a student he regularly robbed apartments and later, in 1948, he killed two women and a six-year-old girl.

He confessed to reaching sexual climax during murders committed during housebreaking. He was judged insane and sentenced to three consecutive life-terms, never to be released.

His childlike script, with downward slope and poorly formed letters, show emotional stress, nervousness and maladjustment.

LEE HARVEY OSWALD

Lee Harvey Oswald is thought to have been the killer of President Kennedy at Dallas in November 1963.

The pressure in Oswald's script varies, indicating emotional instability and inconsistency. The many different formations of his *t* bar crossings show indecisiveness and changing moods varying from undue optimism to depression and confusion.

The leftward swing of his small *g* and *y* and their underlengths indicate a strong mother influence in his early years. His small *d* is enrolled, a sign of his introspective nature, showing he is completely wrapped up in himself. His unusually forward right slant shows lack of emotional control, and the almost illegible signature with high upper loops, reveals his egoism and need to show off, seeking to appear far more important than he is. The name Oswald gets larger at the end and this is a cardinal sign of emotional immaturity.

THOMAS COCHRAN

Thomas Cochran was convicted in the 1950s of murdering a young woman in South Florida, after posing as a movie scout. He too has the pasty, sensual writing so often associated with abnormal sexual appetites and self-interest. The left slant indicates his introverted nature and the blobs reveal his sensuality.

H. JUDD GREY

H. Judd Grey killed the husband of his lover in the 1950s, and here again the muddy script reveals strong sexuality and an exceedingly weak will. His forward right script indicates an impulsiveness that led to the murder.

IAN BRADY

Brady's signature – 1965.

O.B	DET	CARR	STM	END
HAT	Clean before wipe, to place in paper container which has been cleaned...... After use replace in container.	X		Burn shaft bury head.
CAR	Remove all moveable objects, clean cover floor and seat fresh Poly. at night. Co-ord all moveables keys etc		X	Destroy Poly. inspect car for spots.
GN	Polish, Bulls Polish.	X		Dave
TICK	Place P/B.		X	
PIEC	Check periodically unmoved			W/H
PRO P	STIMULATE	-		
CIARR	for Hutch, haplis log			Destroy

Brady's disposal plan for getting rid of his victims' bodies – 1966.

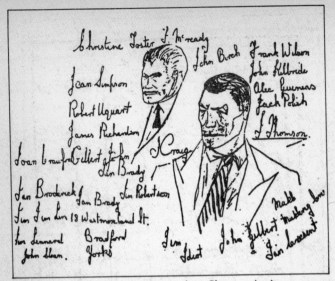

Brady's scribbles during the trial at Chester Assizes –
6 May 1966.

Ian Brady's small, right-slanted script with its good
spacing shows intelligence, organising ability and an
eye for detail. The lack of loops indicates his poverty
of emotion and the left-slanted starting stroke to
some of his capitals reveals the strong influences
from the past that still haunt him.

The downward slope of his lines is a sign of
depression and the small middle-zone letters reveal
his ability to concentrate. They also show that he is
susceptible to feelings of inferiority. The rhythm of
his writing tends to fluctuate indicating that he was
under stress at the time of writing.

There is egoism in the underlined signature and
the way in which he forms his commas and full stops
— long and flung down — gives away his pent-up anger
and frustration.

20/6/87　　　490, I Brady,
　　　　　　　Park Lane Hospital
　　　　　　　Leverpool.

Dear Mr West,
　　　　　　　　Many thanks
for your last letter.
The reason I have not replied
sooner is that many things
that are happening must not
reach the press yet.
I suppose you've seen or heard
that the Home Office, on the
strength of my information, are
re-opening the case.
I can't tell you anything
else. You'll see or read about
it soon.
　　　　　Sincerely,
　　　　　　　　Ian Brady

PS: I'm glad you got in well
with my mother. She knows
nothing at all about the
moors, etc.

Written by Brady to Mrs Ann West – 1987

63

This is the Zodiac speaking

I have become very upset with
the people of San Fran Bay
Area. They have <u>not</u> complied
with my wishes for them to
wear some nice ⊕ buttons.
I promiced to punish them
if they did not comply, by
anilating a full School Bass.
But now school is out for
the summer, so I punished
them in an another way.
I shot a man sitting in
a parked car with a .38.

⊕-12   SFPD-0

The Map coupled with this
code will tell you who-e the
bomb is set. You have antill
next Fall to dig it up. ⊕

C △ J I ■ ● O K ⅃ A M ꟻ ▲ Ω O R T G
X ⊙ F D V ꝯ ⊡ H C E L ⊕ P W △

64

This is the Zodiac speaking
Like I have always said
I am crack proot. If the
Blue Meannies are evere
going to catch me, they had
best get off their fat asses
& do something. Because the
longer they fiddle & fart
around, the more slaves
I will collect for my after
life. I do have to give them
credit for stambling across
my riverside activity, but
they are only finding the
easy ones, there are a hell
of a lot more down there:
The reason that Im writing
to the Times is this, They
dont bury me on the back pages
like some of the others.
SFPD —0   ⊕ —17+

The Zodiac Murders — as they became known —
took place in California during a nine-month period in
1969. The murderer sent letters to the newspapers
signed with a zodiac cross over a circle. There were

five murders in all, two teenagers shot dead in their car, a taxi driver shot, and another couple. The murderer kept up a correspondence with the newspapers until 1974. The Zodiac Murders remain unsolved.

Again in the sample of the Zodiac murderer's handwriting we see the same heavy, smeary writing and pressure seen in so many samples of handwriting where the writer has sexual problems of a sadistic or perverted nature. The handwriting becomes more angular at the bottom of the page and the right slant more pronounced as he becomes excited while writing.

THE HANGMAN: ALBERT PIERREPOINT

Albert Pierrepoint, the hangman, inherited his job from his father Henry and his uncle Tom and carried out the last ritual of his trade in 1956 when he retired for reasons that are still secret. A few years later the death penalty for murder in this country was abolished, and on 23 August 1964 the last two executions were carried out simultaneously in Liverpool and Manchester.

Pierrepoint was responsible for despatching many murderers to their death, among the most notorious Hanratty the A4 murderer, Christie the necrophiliac killer, Heath the sadist, Haigh the acid bath murderer, and Edith Thompson who was hanged with her lover Frederick Bywaters for the murder of her husband in 1923. The last woman to be hanged in Britain was Ruth Ellis in July 1955 for the shooting of her ex-lover.

Pierrepoint was also responsible for hanging many of the war criminals at Nuremburg.

In the handwriting of this ex-public executioner the symbols of his trade can be seen in the noose formation in his upper loops on the letters *R* and *P*. He also forms his *t* bar crossing in a way that resembles a gallows.

The right slant of his script indicates that he is a socially minded man, with great self-reliance. He can be outgoing and friendly but this is offset with a tinge of reserve, as he is, in fact, a very private person. He also shows in the large loop at the left of his capital *A* that he is a man proud of his family and his and their achievements.

3

Hoax letters

Dear Officer,
                                                    March 23rd 78
            Sorry I havn't written, about a year to be
exalt, but I havn't been up North for quite a while.
I was'nt kidding last time I wrote

                                                            That
was last month, so I don't know when I will
get back on the job but I know it wont be
Chapeltown too bloody hot there maybe
Bradford, Manningham. Might write again
if up North.
                        Jack the Ripper
P.S Did you get letter I sent to Daily Mirror
in Manchester.

69

These hoax letters sent during the search for the so-called 'Yorkshire Ripper', indicate that the writer was a man of considerable energy and anger. This is seen in the heavy pressure, forward slant, and lack of control in the wavering baseline.

The straightforward *I* shows that his intelligence is above average, and he gets down to essentials quickly. The form level shows him to be a manual worker perhaps, or an artisan with a knowledge of the skill of writing.

The pointed downstrokes to his letters are a sign of aggression, and the varying slant indicates instability in the emotional area.

August 16th

Dear John

Tried to phone you up at weekend but couldn't get you. Also tried on Monday. It was a pity I couldn't get in touch as I'm sure you'd have liked to have come as something happened of interest.

Perhaps you could come to the club one night and I'll put you in the picture. Any night will do but as I am off work perhaps Thursday night.

I'll turn up this time, not like last week. I only just missed you thag I saw you riding off

Yours
The Caller

This is a hoax letter sent to the wife of a man who had rejected the writer, who had formed an unhealthy attachment to him. The writer is obsessed by the recipient of this letter and there are strong sexual symbols in the phallus-shaped upper loops. Combined with the raised *t* bar crossings they also show that a sense of unreality is causing extreme agitation.

4

Political and war criminals

BENITO MUSSOLINI

The left slant shows his introverted tendencies and that he was suppressed emotionally, while the pointed sharpness of his letters indicate his aggression and lack of tolerance. The repressed style of his script shows obsessional behaviour patterns, and those arcade formations indicate concealment and caution. He is not going to let anything stop him from achieving his aims. They also demonstrate suspicion and that he is under enormous pressure.

ADOLF HITLER

The sample of Hitler's signature in 1933, just before he became Reich-Chancellor, has a tendency to fall downwards towards the end, indicating that he suffered from considerable depression, and was not a particularly optimistic personality.

Both this and his later signature have a right slant with varying pressure and sharp knife-like crossings that also descend, emphasising his manic depressive state.

His signatures are made up of angles, always a sign of rigid and compulsive thinking, without care for the opinion or the views of other people.

There are signs of sudden and eruptive emotional outbursts in his writing, and in the second signature one can observe the swastika, the emblem of Hitler's notorious bodyguard.

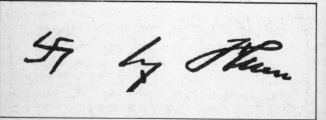

Even allowing for the fact that German writing is, and was even more so in the thirties, much more angular and rigid than English script, Himmler has narrow and controlled angularity that shouts of aggression and a complete lack of warmth or emotion. The razor-like strokes breathe of intolerance and a calculated coldness with sadistic tendencies and an ability to carry orders out without qualm. This is a typical example of the schizoid personality.

RUDOLF HESS

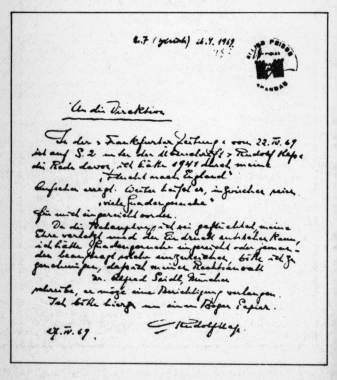

Compared with Himmler's signature, Hess has far more rounded writing, a right slant, and better release of tension in the broader formations of his letters. He also reveals some altruism in the closeness of his words, indicating his ability to work with others, and that he has a need to communicate.

There are no signs in his signature of the in-built sadism or aggression evident in Himmler's signature, and from his writing Hess shows a healthy respect for duty and conventionality.

5

Rapists

Crime statistics show that during the last ten years the number of cases of rape has shot up alarmingly, as has murder after rape. The handwriting of men who have committed this particular crime, not surprisingly, shows a strong sex drive which is revealed in the form of the small g's and y's but it is difficult to generalise. There are countless men with a strong sex drive, but they have self-control and are not obsessed.

When these strong instinctive urges are seen in the handwriting of young people, their physical energy can be channelled into sport, games or other physical activities, and turned to good advantage. When this energy is repressed, it can erupt and lead to attacks on women.

When there is heavy pressure and pasty writing, it indicates someone more concerned with the purely sensual and physical.

H. M. PRISON,
St. LOYES,
BEDFORD.

3rd. November 1965

Dear Sir,

Sorry to have to write you a letter from a prison, but I am up to my neck in trouble.

I'm asking you a favour on behalf of my Solicitor, that would you give me a working report a reference if you like.

Either I am a bad bricklayer or a good one.

I know I had my ups and downs with the firm. But I was not sacked, I left and went on for Monks, Hills Road Bridge I think you will remember.

It would be greatly appreciated if you would do that for me. I always tried to do my best for the firm.

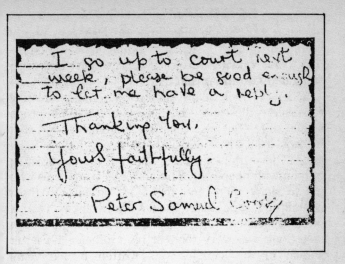

Peter Samuel Cook, aged 47, was sent to prison in October 1975 after being found guilty on six charges of rape at Cambridge.

Cook had a history of crime since the age of ten, and had many convictions for burglary. He was sent to Broadmoor in 1966, was released two years later and went to live in Cambridge. He got married but his wife knew nothing of his sexual urges.

In 1980 Cook tried to smuggle letters out of Parkhurst Prison on the Isle of Wight, to a national newspaper, in which he pleaded for assistance to obtain a sex-change operation. He also sent photographs of himself in female clothing. These pictures had been taken with a camera which had been smuggled into the prison.

When we look at his handwriting, it is interesting to observe the traits that not only reveal his strong sexual urges but also feminine tendencies, and that he was from his youth under a strong female influence. These traits are often found in the handwriting of men with deep-rooted homosexual tendencies who try to deny them and this leads in fact to them committing rape and assaults on women. This is often associated with a dominant mother influence. In fact Cook was very fond of his mother. The letter shown in the samples was written twelve years before he was committed for trial on charges of rape. The single signature was written at the time of the charges.

6

Anonymous letter writers

A skilful and fluent writer can quite easily assume a copybook hand and get away with it, but a slow and semi-literate writer can never disguise his lack of education by writing a quick and cultivated hand.

When an outbreak of anonymous letters occurs, one looks for motive words — that is, names or words that have been written a little heavier than the rest of the script, and which obviously have a significant meaning to the writer. They can signify anger, hate, emotion or malice, but they do give away the writer's thoughts and indicate sometimes where the writer may be found, and why he or she has a grudge against someone and has to libel them.

The anonymous letter writer forgets that speed, pressure, spacing between words, letters, lines and margins all reveal to the graphologist, with amazing accuracy, a great deal about the writer's personality. When there are letters with which to compare the anonymous letters, then the culprit is quite easily spotted.

EXAMPLE 1

Oct 2rd.   R. S. P. C. A.

Animal

neglected . Badly

hut soaking wet

calling back _____

All the occupants of houses in an entire road of a London suburb received anonymous letters over a period of twenty years, causing considerable distress and misery to the recipients, many of whom were elderly or ill. The letters were not obscene, or threatening, but lying, stupid and hurtful. Their malicious contents indicated the vicious nature of the mean and spiteful person who was penning them.

An elderly woman was suspected by neighbours and the police were alerted, but they could do

> Please
>
> see that your lovely cat is taken
> in at night Im not saying the letter name
> it wont cause any unpleasoness I ask the
> young lady near you because I thought
> it was her cat she said no she has no pets
> because of her mother.
> I heard it wont stay in its not true its
> has slept here with one for two days im
> moving and I wouldnt like to know its
> neglected
>
>   sorry its so lovely

nothing as no one was seen actually to deliver the letters, as they were always posted from a nearby town. The writing was compared with the script of the suspect and it was confirmed that she was indeed the anonymous letter writer. However, since she was old and ill she was not prosecuted.

The letters reproduced here reveal the writer is suffering from resentment, anger, frustration and jealousy and seems to be of slow and limited intelligence. The basic character structure of the writer is clear — the writing shows signs of senile decay, a narrow-minded hypersensitive personality with a highly developed critical sense.

The badly formed letters are a sign of a poorly educated writer with low intelligence. The pressure (in the animal welfare letter in particular) shows that it was written in extreme anger and under tension.

> WE THOUGHT YOU SHOULD NO THAT YOUR NEXT DOOR
> NEIGHBOURS THERE NOT HUSBAND OR WIFE HE HAD A NICE
> WIFE AND TWO CHILDREN HE LEFT HIS WIFE TO
> LIVE WITH HER AND SHE MADE HIM PUT
> THEM IN DOCTOR BARNODOES HOME AND THEY
> ARE TWO NICE CHILDREN SHE IS A BAD LOT SHE
> IS A BOASTER TWISTER AND A FILTHY LIAR ALL
> THAT HOME WHAT SHE AS GOT IS NOT PAID FOR
> WE ALL NO WHAT SHE IS SHE HAD A GOOD
> HUSBAND BUT HE WAS NOT ENOUGH FOR HER
> SHE IS A EVIL WICKED JEALLOUS WOMAN SHE
> CAN DRINK A BOTTLE OF JIN WHILE YOUR A
> DRINKING A GLASS OF WATER WE ALL ISNOW
> HER OF OLD THEY ALL NO HER UP THE PRINCESS
> BOWL IN FACT SHE IS WELL NOWN OVER GALE ST
> AND HE IS NOT MUCH BETTER FOR HE AS A NASTY
> NAME IN A WORKING MANS CLUB AT MILL RD
> AVELEY AND A LOT OF CLUBS NO WHAT THEY
> ARE ESPECIALY HER .

The script of the letter written in capitals demonstrates the immature nature of the writer; the letters increase in size at the ends of words — a sign of immaturity — and under close scrutiny the letter formations show the same physically disintegrating strokes to be seen in the RSPCA letter.

The writer is living in a world of inner conflicts and partly because of her lack of physical energy and vitality she feels inadequate. Curiously, the rising lines show optimism and that the writer has an exaggerated ego that must keep everything immaculate.

EXAMPLE 2

Now peter because you were ½ 8 '76
an amateur prize fighter, funny a
few mins's aboud you clouted an officer
of the law you adopted a welsh name
I gather peter you could be a mixed breed
as in wales and england for generations
the suffosed english and welsh scum
like your self are polish decent and
slaves Belgiuns and Balkan states the
man you assulted could be of the same
breed as you and a million welsh men
and 4 million in the english countries and
cities here in london they are all foreigns
say 8 emillian you neredninnk when
you struck that policeman whet were
you doing there any way you Bostord
you would not get away with there
here in england you dirty low bred
scum the foles in your church make
you are a hero do me a favour peter
place you head in a gas oven or Jump
under a Heavy vehicle you and your
half bred chinese jezzebe girl friend
I pray for your death you Bastord
you will not go there in a Hurry
again thy should hove esclcuted
Both of you scum I am inviting the
government of that country when you
Read this note you'll laugh peter alias Dewey
you are on the spot you'll die soon
from I steban you are cnot a penny Saint

87

This writer is extremely unbalanced as shown in the fluctuating slant and baseline. There are signs of a guilt complex and of aggression and hostility towards himself as seen in numerous swings to the left in the loops of the letters. The word 'executed' is a little larger than the rest of his script, and is what is known as the motive word, emphasising his obsession with it.

He has found a way of expressing his resentment against everything and everybody in a negative way by putting pen to paper and writing abuse.

There are indications that the writer is a latent homosexual though it is possible that it was written by a masculine woman. The underlengths to the small *g* and *y* are swinging to the left — the mother fixation sign in graphology, and the open *a* and *o* indicate that he is talkative, needs to be with people, lacks discretion, and is obstinate to the point of stupidity.

The wavering base line shows his inconsistent personality and moodiness, being up one day and down the next, and also his nervous energy which finds expression in sudden bursts of irritability under tension.

7

Spies

Here are five examples of notorious traitors. I have studied the signatures of the following:

- Dr Klaus Fuchs, the atomic scientist who betrayed secrets to the Russians while working at the Atomic Energy Establishment at Harwell. Fuchs was arrested in 1950.
- Kim Philby, perhaps the most famous and certainly one of the most successful of all British traitors.
- Guy Burgess, who vanished with Philby in 1951.
- Anthony Blunt, Surveyor of the Queen's Pictures, whose treachery was exposed in 1978.
- John Vassal, clerk to the Naval Attache in Moscow, gaoled for spying in September 1950.

The signatures of these men of treachery and deceit all have the same things in common — they reveal intelligence (often of the highest order), clever skill at manipulation, concealment and social graces.

FUCHS

Klaus Fuchs

His signature is small, simplified and without ostentation. It shows mental agility, analytical skill and well-developed powers of manipulation in the thread-like strokes.

PHILBY

Kim Philby

Philby's signature is pressured showing quite a thick script, indicating his sensuality and a love of good food, wine and the luxuries of life. He, too, eliminates loops and non essential additions to his name and the exact placing of his *i* dots reveals his excellent eye for detail.

BURGESS

Guy Burgess has intelligence and a lurking arrogance in his signature. The step-like names show mood variation and there's more than a hint of melancholy in his signature. A critical observer, not a lot of moral strength and an underlying feeling of mild inferiority compensated for by intellectual self-confidence.

BLUNT

Blunt has a very lightly pressured script showing his hypersensitive nature and again we see the thread-like strokes dwindling into a line demonstrating his ability to adapt and be all things to all people. He is careful, cautious, secretive, but also a man with a strong ego as the underlining of his signature shows.

John Vassall

Good head control is seen in the upright script and intelligence in the small letters. His capital letters reveal personal vanity and his writing demonstrates simplicity and intuition developed to a high degree in the breaks between his letters.

8

Young male offenders

The following four samples of handwriting belong to young male offenders. They are written on prison notepaper, which is lined, so the actual baseline is probably different from the baseline they might employ on unlined paper, but the characteristics are similar in all four specimens, both in style and form.

Almost all have high ascenders indicating that the writers live in an unrealistic world of fantasy and dream of making it 'big'. Their aspirations are often not within their capabilities.

EXAMPLE 1

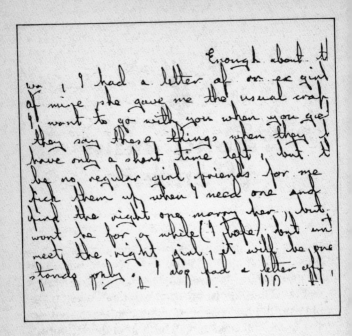

This writer shows strong homosexual tendencies in the left slant of his small *g*'s and *y*'s. The angle strokes reveal his hostility and yet he has a need to communicate and mix as his right slant demonstrates. The elongated *i* dots are a sign of sensitivity and resentment against criticism. The small, fast writing however, shows that he is not without intelligence.

EXAMPLE 2

Dear Sir,

I am writing to you
hope that your firm would
be represent me in my pres
difficulties, which at presen
many and varied and garant
to raise your blood pressure

recall a conversation befor

Again we see high ascenders but this writer is confused and highly emotional with a strong sex drive showing in the long underlengths. He is unable to distinguish what is important and what isn't, will rush into situations without thought for the consequences, and his overwhelming emotional responses lead him to fling himself into the environment and relationships. The poor spacing reveals uncontrolled impulses and irresponsible behaviour due to fluctuating moods.

EXAMPLE 3

You aee ane eny —
to get this book.
I received the comien viberby thank
I also got the book "the flying Roll" from
RP Blackpool. Thankyou also for this.
The reason I took so long to write I wo
see the assistant Governor to ask how lo

A weak ego is seen in this badly formed and pathetic capital *I*. The left slant indicates that the writer is against the world and is withdrawn. Yet the speed and the small script show that he is reasonably intelligent. The ending stroke to his capital *M* gives away his vanity and dislike of compromise.

EXAMPLE 4

If you like it, however, perhaps you write to me direct.

Yours sincerely,

This writer is a showman and his writing displays a lot of vanity in the slightly flourished strokes. The heavy pressure is a sign of energy and drive and there is more than a hint of aggression in the small scythe-like small *d*'s. The ending stroke of his capital *M* going down into the next zone shows his vanity and lack of compromise.

9

Female criminal handwriting

A Home Office research study reveals that the rate of violent crime by women in this country has gone up over 200 per cent in the past few years. Prostitution has almost been taken off the statute book and few women are jailed for this offence.

At any one time in this country, there are only 4,000–5,000 women and girls in prison or borstals although crimes against the person have increased, and so has theft and violence.

The background of many women criminals leaves a lot to be desired and certainly a history of deprivation and even abuse and conflict in the home doesn't help. Many of these women come from environments where petty crime is often the norm.

The following samples of handwriting belong to various types of offender. As we look at their handwriting and read a brief history of each one, we can see in their script some of the reasons why they acted the way they did.

One crime on the increase is drug-pushing, but

over the years the murder of a child by a woman is rare. Weakness, anger, revenge, frustration or just plain greed are the motivations the graphologist looks for — and finds — in their handwriting.

MURDERER

her dolphin and rides around on it, holding onto the fins!

Docter Brunning brought me here by car, for Section 60, and there are two villas or houses, with a family atmosphere.

Please give my regards to Father Pink who was saying a special prayer for me today.

This writer found out that her husband was having affairs with other women and threw his four-year-old son over a bridge to punish him.

There are conflicting slants and poor rhythm in her handwriting showing erratic impulses and energy. The small writing indicates that she is reasonably intelligent but there is a sense of isolation from the environment in the wide spacing.

The weakly hung small g's and y's reveal her fatigue, and low vitality is seen in the lack of pressure. The writing has no drive or motivation, it is weak and ineffectual, and any anger has burnt itself out.

SHOPLIFTER

> of you and the officers as well and would you kindly give them all my best regards,
>
> well dear this is all for now hoping to hear from you,

This writer is a regular inmate of prison and psychiatric hospitals.

The writing shows light pressure indicating physical weakness and a highly sensitive nature. The writer is quick to take offence against slights — real or imaginary — and the lack of energy and erratic script with its varying slants show her to be easily influenced and impressionable.

PROSTITUTE

> I do hope that
> now you are in Hospital
> your arm is feeling more
> comfortable, that it
> will not be long before you
> are out & about again
>
> You will have to
> be very careful when you
> walk across the centre
> in future, won't you?

A regular offender, frequently ending up in prison, she looked upon her convictions as part of the price she had to pay.

The distorted underlengths of her small g's and y's show her sexual attitude is ambiguous, with lesbian overtones. The left-turning stroke in the form of an arc-like claw stroke reveals a love of money and an avoidance of responsibility. The right slant indicates her social attitude is outgoing and the large capital *I* again, with an arc, means that she has a somewhat exaggerated ego compensating for feelings of inferiority.

should have stopped my nonsense

and should have worked at

Hollower Prison. While I have been

at Broadmoor Hospital I have

knitted a blanket and I am now

beginning to make rings. Super fun!

And, of course, they may be useful

when I leave Broadmoor Hospital

and have to start a new home.

Actually, I am still longing for a

This writer killed her mother after great provocation. She spent five years in Broadmoor and then went on to psychiatric homes. She is afraid to grow up and has attempted suicide.

The very high upper loops show she lives in a fantasy world. The narrow script indicates clearly her inhibited nature which is the result of emotional and environmental repression in her youth causing difficulty in releasing tension. The low *t* bar crossing is a sign of depression and the upright script shows her feelings are held rigidly in check.

THIEF

This writer was in and out of prison for theft from an early age. A persistent shoplifter, she was also aggressive and had a tendency to drink too much.

The left slant of her handwriting reveals introspection due to past experiences and influences in her early life. The open base to her small *a*'s and *o*'s are classic signs of dishonesty. These traits are frequently found in the writing of con men or people who live on their wits.

The shaky writing shows the influence of alcohol and the poorly developed rhythm in the structure of the letters shows nervousness. The slow script and lack of drive signifies a laconic personality who may easily take the line of least resistance.

PSYCHOPATH

This writer is intelligent but uneducated. She was diagnosed as a psychopath and has been in and out of custody for grievous bodily harm. Her main crime was wounding with a knife.

The heavy pressure of the writing reveals her anger and pent-up frustrations. The fluctuating slant and inability to maintain a straight baseline shows her poor discipline. There is a sharp temper in the angular strokes and sharpened *t* bars. The filled in letters show uncontrolled sensuality. The small badly formed capital *I* is a sign of an inferiority complex, yet the writing has a certain amount of originality. It demonstrates a complete lack of emotional and mental stability and the writer will act unpredictably and without thought for the consequences.

ARSONIST

I say it my-self, quess I
have changed one way and
another, but one thing is
Certain, I'll never get married
its not my Scene, old fasioned
anyway, when it all boils
down its money spent on
buying a cage, and Ive
had enough of being a
bird in a quilded Cage,
no more Cage's for me mrs
██████, do give my love to
MRS ██████ ██████, miss ████
yes I remember miss ████████
ask her if she remembers

This writer had fifteen convictions for various crimes before she was seventeen. After attempting to burn down a house she was sent to a mental hospital to recover and suddenly began to get better after meeting an old friend. She set up house with him after coming out of hospital and settled down.

Her handwriting reveals her emotional immaturity in the copybook script and slow speed. The left slant shows her difficulty in establishing relationships. Her inability to mix and communicate is confirmed by the large spaces between her words. The heavy pressure indicates energy and crude sensuality.

These other examples of female offenders follow:

CONSTANCE KENT

Constance Kent, at 21 years old, confessed to killing her half-brother five years earlier. She had been suspected of murdering the four-year-old at the time and was arrested, but later released on her father's bond of £200. She entered a convent in France and after two-and-a-half years moved to a convent in Brighton. Her religious beliefs led her to confess. She was sent for trial at Salisbury Assizes in 1865, pleaded guilty and was sentenced to death without a witness being called. The sentence was commuted to life imprisonment and she was released in 1885.

Even allowing for the flourishes in her script which were popular and very much in evidence in handwriting in the last century, this writing shows a healthy ego and a very strong suppressed sexuality. The wide margin on the left is a sign of her fear about the past and indicates her desire to keep the world at bay as much as possible.

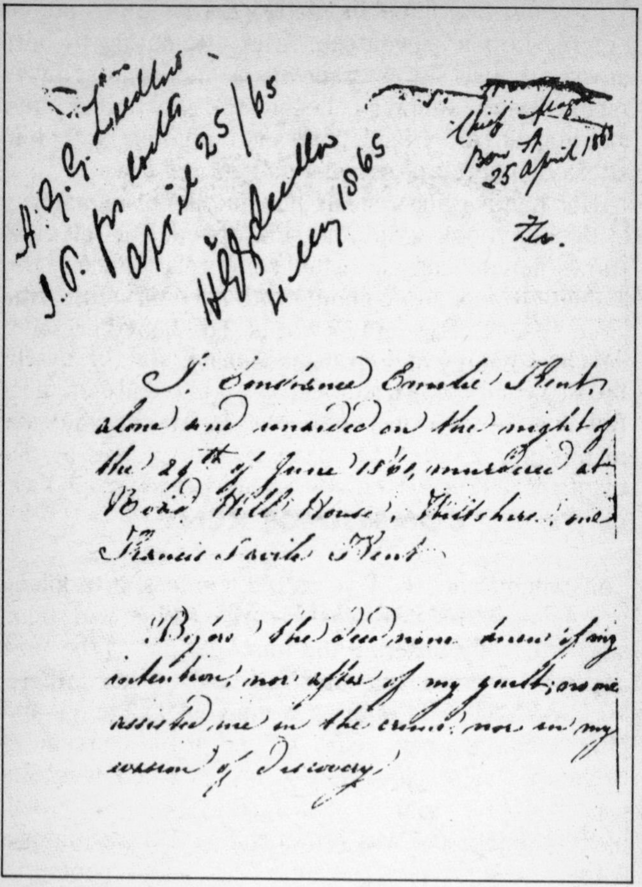

[handwritten signatures and notations at top]

A.G.G. Ludlow
J.P. for Wilts April 25/65

H.G.G. declow [?] 4 may 1865

this A.E.
Bow St
25 April 1865
Ho.

[handwritten statement]

I, Constance Emelie Kent, alone and unaided on the night of the 29th of June 1860, murdered at Road Hill House, Wiltshire, one Francis Savile Kent.

"Before the deed none knew of my intention; nor after of my guilt; no one assisted me in the crime; nor in my evasion of Discovery."

Excellent organising ability is shown in her spacing and the huge inflated capital reveals vanity and arrogance.

AMELIA DYER

Amelia Dyer, in 1896, was responsible for the deaths by drowning of a number of young children near Reading. The thickness of her strokes reveals a brutal disposition, as does the pasty or muddy appearance of her letters in which the endings are abruptly cut off. Her motive was gain.

MADELAINE SMITH

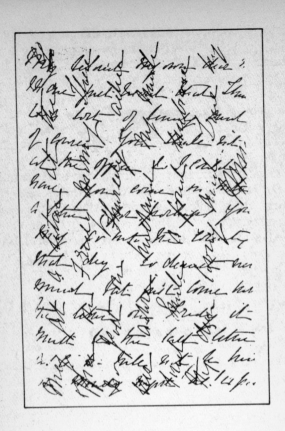

'Not Proven' is the Scottish verdict indicating 'We think you did it — don't do it again.' In July 1887 Madelaine Smith, 22-year-old daughter of wealthy Glasgow businessman James Smith, was acquitted by the jury on a verdict of 'Not Proven', on the charge of poisoning her lover Emile L'Angelier. Smith was accused of administering arsenic to him after accepting an offer of marriage from another man her family approved of. L'Angelier had been a passionate Frenchman who refused to let her go, and Smith was certainly not the innocent party she presented at her trial. Her love letters sent ripples through the sedate Glasgow middle class community.

The angles in her writing show aggression and critical mindedness. There is pent-up passion and impulsiveness in the hasty right-slanted script but the spiky strokes and sharp tips of her loops indicate cruelty. The long extended end strokes reveal an intolerant nature and a desire to escape the routine of respectability. They are also an egotistical sign, so is the large signature with its underlining. The long lower loops show her materialistic leanings and sexuality.

10
Myra Hindley

up'. That's just how I feel at the moment... Something
dying inside me, and it's the will to live. Although I
subscribe to Nietzsche's 'he who has the why to live is
any how', at the same time, I feel like the prisoner
talks about, when he said: "Woe to him who sees
_no_ aim, no purpose, and therefore no point in carrying
on last." I don't know whether it is because of acute
makes me feel, deep in my heart, that I'll never be let
out until I'm quite old. I feel tortured with grief at
~~the disaster~~ I have caused, and I can hardly live with
I just want to drag myself into a corner, in the dark,
and where it knows it is dying, and if I had no moral re
let ~~me~~ once so much to so many people, I think I
easily do so now. But not for the next few years,

Hindley was imprisoned for life in May 1966 with her lover Ian Brady, for the murder of Lesley Ann Downey aged ten, and Edward Evans aged seventeen. She was convicted as an accomplice to the murder of John Kilbride as well. The case was known as 'The Moors Murders'.

Myra Hindley has an almost childlike script which is legible and carefully formed. But the small size of her writing and the capital *I* made in a single stroke downwards shows intelligence and a quick grasp of essentials. She is able to assess situations at a glance. The basic left slant is often seen in the handwriting of those who are against society rather than for it. When seen in female handwriting it demonstrates a masculine mind and occasionally cold-bloodedness, promiscuity, secretiveness and insincerity. The narrow spaces between her words demonstrate her need to be with people; this need is almost pathological.

The dots over the small *i* when elongated reveal touchiness and hypersensitivity under criticism. The light pressure of the writing is a sign of sensitivity. The middle zone letters are neglected compared with the loops and underlengths and show that home and family feelings seem to be negative. The open underlengths to her small *g*'s and *y*'s indicate an extremely receptive and responsive personality in the erotic/ sexual sphere, but a person who is gullible and emotionally ambivalent. When the loop of the *g* and *y* are not crossed but open to the left, this is a sign of immaturity. The thick *t* bar crossing is an indication of obstinacy under tension. She is imaginative, responds to new ideas and projects, is capable of organised study or research and possesses persistence for sustained effort.

The rhythm of the writing looks reasonably stable

until we look at the 'wavy' or slightly 'bent' formation of her upper loops. Even her small *h*'s and capital *l*'s have this particular trait. This noticeable stroke is found in the handwriting of individuals suffering from mental disturbances or conflict due to anxiety. To the trained eye of the graphologist it indicates weakness of will and an easily led personality — a person who will take the easy way out of situations, who leads an active inner life hiding behind a camouflage like a chameleon, and adapts herself to every individual she contacts.

The fact that she does not join her letters in a normal manner, shows a desire to be different, to keep apart and conceal what she does not wish the world to see. The closed small *a*'s and *o*'s confirm her secretiveness.

The disconnected script shows inventiveness and difficulty in fitting in. This type of script shows individuality and a strong desire to live a different lifestyle from others. There is isolation and a capacity for ignoring the normal practical and moral codes of behaviour. The following samples span a period of 25 years. It is rare to see so little change in a handwriting over such time, especially under such circumstances. It is clear that her basic characteristics haven't changed at all, despite her traumatic experiences.

Hindley enjoys notoriety and has a need to project her image in order to boost her ego. She is highly intuitive, as the break between her letters shows, and knows how to play on human nature and is quick to use her considerable insight into weakness. Highly sensitive and with a well-developed critical sense, she leads an active inner life — hiding behind a façade of adaptability. She changes her personality to suit each person she comes into contact with.

She hasn't altered over the years but is still

devious, self-absorbed and clever enough to outwit the world. She has developed her intellectual capacity with a remarkable degree of success but her writing shows her to be suffering from mental disturbances that are causing a great deal of conflict.

Memoirs of a Madman - Alexei Tolstoy. ...
Death's Jest Book - Beddoes.
Axels Castle - Edmund Wilson.
A Vision'. W.B. Yeats.,-
Tales of Good & Evil. W.B. Yeats.. ,.
Caligula & Cross Purposes. A. Camus. .— ... -
Philosophy of Solitude - J. Cowper Powys.
The Haunted Woman - David Lindsay. ,, ...
The Sun in the Sands- Henry Williamson.
Meditations - Marcus Aurelius.
Philosophical Dictionary - Voltaire. .. ... ,,
The Romantic Agony - Mario Praz.
Being & Having., Gabriel Marcel... ,. ,. ..
A Voyage to Arcturus. David Lindsay. .,.
Anatomy of Melancholy - Robert Burton.
Discourses — . Machaivelli.. .—.
Complete Works of T-S. Eliot, including Rhapsody on a Windy Night.
City of Dreadful Night. = James Thompson.
Journey to the End of the Night. - F. L. Celine.
Memoirs of a Happy Lover - Groucho Marx.
Life & Letters of the Brontes, anything on the Brontes

A book list written by Hindley when she was 25.

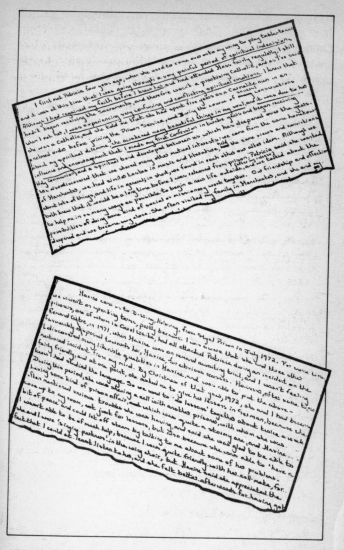

A letter to the parole board after her affair with Patricia Cairn was discovered, 1972.

intelligent and articulate, and as you and I know, she can be a veritable dynamo when she wants to be - and more importantly, when she has to be. So please tell her to keep on keeping on, no matter how hard the going is. Each time the avalanche crushes her, she must do as I have to do; struggle to her feet again, and plod on. The going will be arduous and exhausting - and I'm speaking from experience - but the law of averages (which I don't believe in, but don't tell Debbie that!) must surely mean that circumstances will change for the better. When I've been down - and, in the words of Jim Morrison, I've been down so goddamn long, it feels like up to me - I've always thought of Debbie, of how strong she is (I will not say was, because there's strength even in weakness) and how she was such a pillar of support to me, and I take down her card and read it; she wrote 'In the midst of winter I suddenly learned There was in me An invincible summer.' Now tell her those words have been an inspiration to me, so they must inspire her; they're her own words, and that word invincible is the key word. When battered by all the weapons used against us in one form or another, we have to be invincible, and strive to be impervious to them. As Spike Milligan said, life is one long illness, curable only by death - but death is the

Private letter written in 1989.

easy way out at all the hassles, and no matter how
we feel, we have to live on. I came from a visit with
Mike yesterday (Fri;); I haven't been sleeping - maybe
2-3 hours, then I'm up all night, brooding, thinking,
writing letters to stop myself from thinking too much
about copping out of existence - and the things Mike
and I had to discuss weren't what one would describe
as edifying. I was almost sleepwalking as I crawled
up the stairs, and I almost crashed into Fr. John
as he was approaching his office. He asked me how I
was. I said 'I wish I could celebrate Christ's
birthday with Him, in heaven, instead of having to
remain down here in this vale of tears.' I've no
way out - I can't commit the mortal sin of suicide
and I can't leave an unbearable legacy of pain
to my poor mother and others who love me. So
tell Debbie to remember that unbearable legacy
of pain she'd leave her parents with, and everyone
else who loves her so dearly. She also wrote on
her card 'My heart and sinews cry out for justice
- therefore it will be achieved - it must be
achieved. With you always, Deborah.' Remind her
of those words, Dora. I don't believe in British
justice any more (and I'm not referring to my
own situation when I say that, because the rags
determine injustice for me), but I do believe in
justice as a concept, and in Debbie's case, she
who has suffered so much injustice - her heart

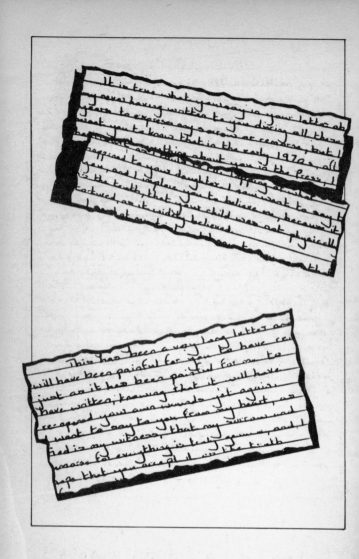

A letter written to victim Lesley Ann Downey's mother, 1988.

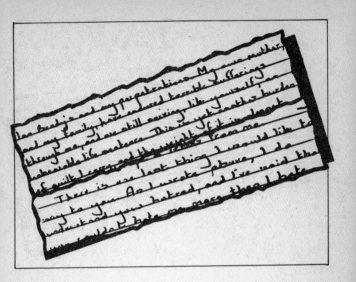

11

Murder or Accident?

Somewhere in Britain — possibly the South Coast town of Bournemouth in Dorset — is a man or woman living with a terrible secret. They have kept that secret for five long years, since a night in 1986 when something happened leaving them with an overwhelming sense of fear and guilt.

Sandra Court was a lively 27-year-old clerk with the Abbey National Insurance Company in Bournemouth. She had just left her job and was going to take up a post as nanny to the children of a hotel owner in Spain. She celebrated with her friends at a night-club called Steppes.

Sandra left her friends in the early hours of 5 May 1986, a little drunk and unsteady on her feet. She called a taxi to take her to her sister's home where she planned to spend the night. After the taxi left her at the door and had gone, she realized her sister was away that night so was unable to get in. She was last seen walking barefeet along the street at two in the morning. That was the last sighting of her. What happened next must be conjecture, but she obviously started to walk home. Her body was found next morning a few miles outside Bournemouth. She had been strangled with a ligature. The contents of her bag were scattered around several streets. The police carried out extensive enquiries without success, treating her death as murder. A few days later, detectives in charge of the investigation received this anonymous letter.

dear Sir I am writing to tell you that the tragic death of Sandra Court was a complete and utter accident, in no form is the person a killer or murderer the person concerned is deeply unhappy, hurt, and in total shock the only reason the person has not come forward is the fact of being afraid that their explanation will not be believed Please I beg take this letter to be of the truth

As a graphologist I have studied many anonymous letters and, although it is possible to assume different writing styles, it is extremely difficult to disguise your handwriting. There are idiosyncratic features that *cannot* be concealed. This letter is an attempt to hide the writer's script, particularly in the acute left slant but many idiosyncratic features reveal themselves. The following pen-portrait of the writer emerges and is built up from the spacing, pressure, formation, idiosyncratic, and academic features of the individual letters.

The writer is mature, rather than young, has religious leanings and is introverted. He or she has a highly nervous disposition and an 'immaculate ego', is money-minded and thrifty, energetic and painstaking, and is under the dominance of a stronger personality. He or she is emotionally and sexually repressed.

The writer will possess rigidly held views and opinions, finds it hard to adapt and was brought up in a restrictive environment. A well-developed critical sense means that there will be an exaggerated self-control hiding an eccentric craving for aloofness and singularity.

It is necessary to know the age and sex of a writer before attempting to analyse a piece of handwriting. Age because some writers are old at 22, some are still young at 60. Sex because everyone has characteristics of both sexes in their make-up.

Obviously, when an experienced graphologist has been analysing handwriting for a number of years it is possible to be reasonably accurate about the age and sex of the writer. But no reputable graphologist would ever make even an inspired guess. In this sample of handwriting I have not given clues to the characteristics but just a straightforward report on the personality structure of the writer.

Was Sandra Court killed deliberately and cold-bloodedly, or was her death an accident as the writer of the letter claims? The mystery remains one to baffle the police. The writing remains to intrigue the graphologist.

Bibliography

Hearns, Rudolph S., *Handwriting, An Analysis Through its Symbolism*, Vantage Press 1966.

Jacoby, H.J., *Analysis of Handwriting*, George Allen & Unwin 1939.

Jung, Carl, *Four Archetypes*, Routledge & Kegan Paul 1959.

Jung, Carl, *Man and his Symbols*, Picador 1964.

Jung, Carl, *The Integration of the Personality*, Kegan Paul 1940.

Marcuse, Irene, *Applied Graphology*, Macoy Publishing Co. 1960.

Meyer, Oscar, *The Language of Handwriting*, Peter Owen 1960.

Mendel, Alfred O., *Personality in Handwriting*, Stephen Days Press 1974.

Olanova, Nadya, *The Psychology of Handwriting*, Wiltshire 1960.

Olanova, Nadya, *Handwriting Tells*, Peter Owen 1978.

Roman, Klara, *Handwriting, A Key to Personality*, Routledge & Kegan Paul 1964.

Saudek, Robert, *The Psychology of Handwriting*, George Allen & Unwin 1925.

Saudek, Robert, *Anonymous Letters*, Methuen 1933.

Saudek, Robert, *What Your Handwriting Shows*, T. Warner Laurie, 1932.

Singer, Eric, *A Manual of Graphology*, Duckworth 1969.

Singer, Eric, *Personality in Handwriting*, Duckworth 1974.

Sonnermann, Urich, *Handwriting Analysis*, Grune & Stratton 1950.

Wolff, Warner, *Diagrams of the Unconscious*, Grune & Stratton 1950.

THE LADY KILLERS
Jonathan Goodman

The firing of a dainty pistol; the administering of subtle poison; quiet, suspicious deaths in the peaceful countryside. They could be elegant mysteries by Agatha Christie. They're not. They're true stories of famous women murderers – suggesting that the female of the species is deadlier than the male . . .

In THE LADY KILLERS Jonathan Goodman has gathered together a fascinating collection of true tales of murderesses past and present. They include poisoner supreme Mary Elizabeth Wilson, Euphrasie Mercier, a lady's companion who brutally murdered her mistress, Alice Crimmins the suspected child killer, and Jean Harris, notorious for her part in the Scarsdale doctor murder case.

So much for the theory of 'the gentle sex': THE LADY KILLERS will chill all devotees of true crime with its thirteen tales of passion, domestic tragedy and pure cold-blooded murder . . .

Also by Jonathan Goodman in Sphere Books:

THE COUNTRY HOUSE MURDERS
THE SEASIDE MURDERS
THE CHRISTMAS MURDERS
THE RAILWAY MURDERS
THE PLEASURES OF MURDER
THE VINTAGE CAR MURDERS

0 7474 0675 8
CRIME/NON-FICTION

UNNATURAL DEATH
Confessions of a
Forensic Pathologist

Michael Baden M.D.
with
Judith Adler Hennessee

KENNEDY'S AUTOPSY FAILED TO DISCLOSE CRUCIAL EVIDENCE

THE DEATHS OF JOHN BELUSHI AND ELVIS PRESLEY WERE FAR
MORE COMPLEX THAN ANYONE HAS LET ON

DECISIVE MEDICAL FINDINGS IN THE VON BULOW AFFAIR WERE
CONSISTENTLY OVERLOOKED

These are just three of the shocking revelations in Dr
Michael Baden's first-person, no-holds-barred account of
his distinguished career in forensic pathology. Formerly
the Chief Medical Examiner for the City of New York,
he was responsible for determining the causes of tens of
thousands of deaths, from those of presidents and rock
stars to victims of serial killings, perverted sex rituals,
mass disasters, infanticide and drug abuse. In this
compelling and often gruesome expose, he produces
dramatic evidence to demonstrate that political intrigue,
nepotism and professional incompetence have led to
major miscarriages of justice where murder is concerned.

'A book to read through slits between your fingers'
Wall Street Journal

0 7474 0813 0
NON-FICTION

THE KENNEDY CONSPIRACY
Anthony Summers

Action-packed, as readable as a thriller, THE
KENNEDY CONSPIRACY is the definitive book on the
assassination of President Kennedy. Acclaimed on both
sides of the Atlantic, winner of the prestigious Golden
Dagger award for crime non-fiction, it has now been
updated to cover new developments, all of them
disturbing, all of them ignored by officialdom.

* Analyses the French Connection. Two men, one in
jail, one a trusted witness under U.S. Government
protection, have named the gunmen they say killed
Kennedy. Why did the Reagan Justice Department
refuse to pursue the matter?

* Reveals that the Chief of the CIA's Western
Hemisphere Division believed there was a conspiracy,
carried out by 'rogue' colleagues in intelligence.

* Probes evidence that the President's body left Dallas
in one coffin and arrived in Washington in another.

* Reports for the first time the belief of a senior
surgeon who treated the dying Kennedy, that gunmen
fired on the President from two directions.

0 7474 0641 3
NON-FICTION

THE MORMON MURDERS

*Steven Naifeh and
Gregory White Smith*

A TRUE STORY OF GREED, FORGERY, DECEIT AND DEATH . . .

Salt Lake City 1985: In separate attacks, a businessman
and his associate's wife were blown apart by pipe bombs
filled with nails. Then a third bomb severely injured a
rare documents dealer. All three victims were devout
members of the Church of Latter-Day Saints – otherwise
known as the Mormon Church.

The investigation of their deaths uncovers an incredible
story of forgery, fraud, lust and murder that will shock
the world and reveal the true corruption and hypocrisy of
the Mormon Church.

'Compelling . . .'
Chicago Tribune

'A first-rate true-crime thriller'
Detroit Free Press

'Exhaustively researched, engrossingly told'
Kirkus Reviews

0 7474 0558 1
NON-FICTION

UNFRIENDLY SKIES
Captain X and Reynolds Dodson

'There have been mechanics who have been threatened
for reporting mechanical failures. There are pilots at
several airlines who have been censured by their
superiors for having dared to suggest that their planes
might not be airworthy. The inevitable result is that pilots
have learned to protect themselves. We've learned to
shut up, even if it means endangering the flying public'
Captain 'X'

Captain 'X' is a distinguished commercial airline pilot
with over twenty years experience. He is the first to take
us behind the scenes and into the cockpit to show, first
hand, the truth about what is *really* going on in the skies.
He discloses information on:

* Which airlines have the best – and the worst – safety
records.
* The world's most dangerous airports.
* The thousands of 'near-misses' since deregulation.
* Hundreds of disasters in the skies over the last decade.

Honest, informative and unflinching, UNFRIENDLY
SKIES is as controversial as it is important, and is
required reading for anyone who travels by air.

0 7474 0671 5
NON-FICTION

THE MARK OF THE BEAST
Trevor Ravenscroft

For 2,000 years the Spear of Destiny – the sword that
pierced the side of Christ on the cross – has been held by
the rulers of the western world. Herod the Great,
Charlemagne, the Hapsburgs and, most recently and
ominously, Adolf Hitler, have used the legendary powers
invested in the Spear. Powers of both good and evil . . .

Now the Spear lies in full view of all those who wish to
see it, and the spiritual realities which it symbolises are
open to all mankind.

THE MARK OF THE BEAST is the result of years of
research into the history of the Spear and the history of
good and evil in the western world. Research pointing to
a conclusion so nearly reached at the time of World War
II: that the critical phase of the apocalypse will culminate
in the reappearance of the Beast who will achieve total
world conquest where Hitler failed . . .

And only then will the prophesy of the Revelation of St
John be fulfilled:

'All the inhabitants of the earth will worship the
Beast . . .'

And don't miss THE SPEAR OF DESTINY, also
available in Sphere Books

0 7474 0514 X
GENERAL NON-FICTION

All Sphere Books are available at your bookshop or newsagent, or can be ordered from the following address:

Sphere Books,
Cash Sales Department,
P.O. Box 11,
Falmouth,
Cornwall TR10 9EN.

Alternatively you may fax your order to the above address. Fax No. 0326 76423.

Payments can be made as follows: Cheque, postal order (payable to Macdonald & Co (Publishers) Ltd) or by credit cards, Visa/Access. Do not send cash or currency. UK customers: please send a cheque or postal order (no currency) and allow 80p for postage and packing for the first book plus 20p for each additional book up to a maximum charge of £2.00.

B.F.P.O. customers please allow 80p for the first book plus 20p for each additional book.

Overseas customers including Ireland, please allow £1.50 for postage and packing for the first book, £1.00 for the second book, and 30p for each additional book.

NAME (Block Letters) ....

ADDRESS ....

....

☐ I enclose my remittance for _____

☐ I wish to pay by Access/Visa Card

Number ☐☐☐☐☐☐☐☐☐☐☐☐☐☐☐☐

Card Expiry Date ☐☐☐☐